INFORMATION EXPLORER JUNIOR

Maintaining a Positive Digital Footprint

by Jeff McHugh

CHERRY LAKE PUBLISHING · ANN ARBOR, MICHIGAN

A NOTE TO PARENTS AND TEACHERS: Please remind your children how to stay safe online before they do the activities in this book.

CHERRY LAKE Publishing

A NOTE TO KIDS: Always remember your safety comes first!

Published in the United States of America
by Cherry Lake Publishing
Ann Arbor, Michigan
www.cherrylakepublishing.com

Content Adviser: Gail Dickinson, PhD, Associate Professor, Old Dominion University, Norfolk, Virginia

Photo Credits: Cover, ©iStockphoto.com/THEPALMER; page 6, ©Panom Pensawang/Shutterstock.com; page 8, ©Meg007/Shutterstock.com; page 10, ©Sergey Novikov/Shutterstock.com; page 11, ©Asier Romero/Shutterstock.com; page 13, ©ene/Shutterstock.com; page 14, ©aaron belford/Shutterstock.com; page 15, ©Grey Carnation/Shutterstock.com; page 16, ©dotshock/Shutterstock.com; page 19, ©bikeriderlondon/Shutterstock.com; page 20, ©Lilya Espinosa/Shutterstock.com.

Library of Congress Cataloging-in-Publication Data
McHugh, Jeff, author.
  Maintaining a positive digital footprint / by Jeff McHugh.
    pages cm. — (Information explorer junior)
  Summary: "Learn how to step carefully online and avoid leaving a negative trail on the internet" — Provided by publisher.
  Audience: Grades K to 3.
  Includes bibliographical references and index.
  ISBN 978-1-63137-789-1 (lib. bdg.) — ISBN 978-1-63137-809-6 (pbk.) — ISBN 978-1-63137-849-2 (e-book) — ISBN 978-1-63137-829-4 (pdf)
  1. Internet—Safety measures—Juvenile literature. 2. Internet—Social aspects—Juvenile literature. 3. Privacy, Right of—Juvenile literature. I. Title. II. Series: Information explorer junior.
  TK5105.875.I57M3825 2014
  004.67'8—dc23
                                    2014001364

Cherry Lake Publishing would like to acknowledge the work of The Partnership for 21st Century Skills. Please visit *www.p21.org* for more information.

Printed in the United States of America
Corporate Graphics Inc.
July 2014

Table of Contents

CHAPTER ONE

Follow the Trail

Footprints show where someone or something has been.

You are walking in the woods. You look down and see footprints. The footprints are shaped like hooves. They are far apart, so you know a large animal made them. You guess that it was probably a deer. You can follow the footprints to see where the deer went.

People leave footprints on the ground, just like animals do. People also leave footprints online. A digital footprint is a trail you leave on the Internet.

Angie loves to visit all kinds of Web sites. She uses computers, tablets, and phones to connect to the Internet.

Everyone who goes online leaves a digital footprint.

Anytime Angie uses the Internet, she leaves a trail. The things she **posts** online can affect the way people think about her. The sites she visits tell people what she's doing when she's online. Angie tries to leave a trail that shows her good qualities. This is called a positive digital footprint. Angie's digital footprint will be with her forever, so she wants it to show her best traits.

Everyone should be mindful of what they do online.

To get a copy of this activity, visit www.cherrylakepublishing.com/activities.

Try This

You can follow your own trail by searching your **browser** history. A browser allows you to visit Web sites on the Internet. Some popular browsers are Internet Explorer, Google Chrome, and Safari.

Open a browser and visit five different Web sites. Next, find a button or menu titled "History" at the top of your screen. Click on it to see a list of the sites you just visited. You can click on a site in this list to visit it again. What do the sites in your history say about you? What would you think about someone else if you saw these sites in his or her history?

CHAPTER TWO

Parts of a Digital Footprint

Just like your fingerprint, your digital footprint is not like anyone else's.

A digital footprint is like a fingerprint. Each one is **unique**. How? Let's find out by learning how a digital footprint is made.

A digital footprint has two parts. One part is the trail of Web sites you visit. Your browser remembers the sites you visit. Many sites record your visit, too. Some even remember the sites you visit before and after them. Angie watches ballet videos online. Her teacher prefers sites about ancient China. Angie's sister likes sites with football information. Each person leaves a different trail of Web sites.

Many Web sites track who visits them and how often.

Be careful which photos you share online.

Your digital footprint is also made up of the things you share online. There are many ways to share information on the Internet. Angie's favorite activity is writing a blog. Sometimes, she includes photos or videos. Angie's dad likes to write comments to people on social media such as Facebook and Twitter. Her friend Kris spends most of his time creating his own Web site.

Digital footprints are permanent. Once you add something to the Internet, it is very difficult to remove it. Closing a page or deleting a post doesn't mean that it is gone forever. Many sites **archive** everything that people post on them. This means that it still exists somewhere online. People could find it many years in the future. Does that mean you shouldn't share on the Internet? Of course not. The Internet is a terrific way to share and connect with others. You just need to be smart about sharing.

The Internet is an easy way to stay in touch.

Try This

You've learned that the Web sites you visit become part of your digital footprint. Now let's take a look at the other part: the information you share on Web sites.

1. Make a chart with three columns. Write "Text" at the top of the first column. This column is for ideas you shared on blogs, comments you made on Web sites, and things you wrote on social media sites. Write "Photos" at the top of the second column. Write "Videos" at the top of the third column.

2. Search back through your posts on social media, blogs, and other sites. Try to find things that you have shared on the Internet from school or home. Add them to your chart. Which format—text, photos, or videos—did you share most frequently? Which items are positive additions to your digital footprint?

CHAPTER THREE

Think Before You Share

There are countless videos to watch and posts to read online.

Angie thinks of the Internet as a tool to share things with a large audience. She creates a positive digital footprint by making good choices about what she shares. This includes any messages, photos, or videos she posts to Web sites.

Angie always thinks carefully before posting something. People sometimes copy her posts and send them to other people. Angie loves the idea of a lot of people reading her posts. But it also makes her nervous because strangers could see her photos or read her words. She does not want posts that show a bad side of her to spread around the Internet.

You cannot always control what happens to the words or photos you post.

Think of how to represent yourself online in the most positive way.

Angie follows two simple rules before posting:

1. Respect yourself

You should post only messages, photos, and videos that show something positive about you. Something that seems funny now might be embarrassing later. Before you post, ask yourself these questions:

- What does this post say about me?
- Does it reveal too much about me?
- Is this something I want to share with everyone, including strangers?
- What would my parents or teachers think if they saw this post?

Be careful about posting things other people might not want shared.

2. Respect others

Sometimes your posts may involve other people. You might write about a family member on your blog. Maybe you post a photo or video of your friends. You might even comment on another person's post. Make sure you are respectful when posting about others. Ask yourself:

- Would I say this to the person's face?
- How would this post make the person feel if he or she saw it?
- Could someone get the wrong idea about this post?

To get a copy of this activity, visit www.cherrylakepublishing.com/activities.

Try This

Look back at the list of posts you made in the activity on page 12. Ask the questions listed on pages 15 and 16 about each post. Were your posts respectful of yourself and others? What are some ways you could improve your posts in the future?

CHAPTER FOUR

Protect Your Privacy

Keep your information safe from people who might steal it.

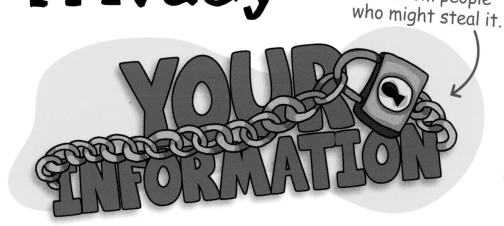

The Internet is a great place for sharing, but you need to be careful not to let strangers know too much about you. You should always keep your personal information private online. Your digital footprint can reveal a lot of information about your life. Strangers could use it to learn about you. Do not share your full name, address, or phone number on the Internet. You should also keep other personal information private, such as your birthday and your school's name.

Many Web sites ask you to choose a **username** before you can post. A username identifies you to others who visit the site. Your username should be a word or phrase that does not include your name, birthday, or other personal information. Use favorite activities or interests instead. Angie loves dancing ballet. She chose "balletstar" as her username. Angie's sister is a big sports fan. She made her username "bearsfan."

Do you love music? Maybe your username could be something to do with that.

You should feel good about the digital footprint you leave behind.

Do not share your usernames and passwords with others. Another person might use your information to log in and pretend to be you. Anything that person posts while logged in as you will affect your digital footprint. By keeping your usernames and passwords private, you control your digital footprint.

Digital footprints can be helpful or harmful. Remember, you are in control of the things you do online. When you use the Internet, protect your privacy and make good choices about what you post. Follow these tips and you will leave a positive digital footprint!

To get a copy of this activity, visit www.cherrylakepublishing.com/activities.

Try This

Choosing a username can be fun! Follow these steps to invent some great (and safe) usernames!

1. Draw a line down the middle of a sheet of paper.
2. On the left side of the page, write down some words that describe you. You might choose words such as *musical*, *funny*, *smart*, or *sporty*.
3. On the right side, write down a list of favorites. Include your favorite hobbies, sports teams, animals, and foods.
4. Match a word from the left with a word from the right to create a unique username, such as "funnytiger." Or add words to your favorites to make "pizzafan" or "fashionstar."

Remember, usernames become part of your digital footprint, so avoid ones that are too silly. The username "stinkymonkey" might seem funny to your friends. However, it may not give others a positive view of you.

Glossary

archive (AHR-kive) to store computer files in a permanent collection

browser (BROU-zur) a computer program that lets you find and look through Web pages and other parts of the Internet

posts (POHSTS) adds words, photos, videos, or other information to the Internet

unique (yoo-NEEK) unlike anything else

username (YOO-zur-naym) a name that you use to identify yourself to a computer, network, or Web site

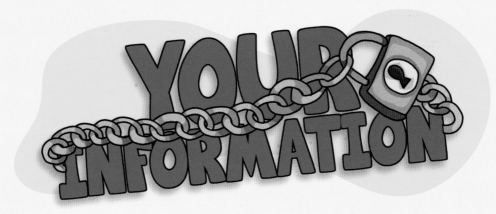

Find Out More

BOOK

Grayson, Robert. *Managing Your Digital Footprint*. New York:
   Rosen Central, 2011.

WEB SITES

BrainPOP—Digital Etiquette
*www.brainpop.com/technology/computersandinternet
/digitaletiquette*
Join Tim and Moby as they explore the importance of using good
manners on the Internet. After watching the video, test your
skills by taking the quiz!

Common Sense Media—Digital Footprint
www.commonsensemedia.org/videos/digital-footprint
This short video explains the importance of making a positive
digital footprint.

Index

About the Author

Jeff McHugh, formerly a second-grade teacher and school librarian, now works as an instructional coach, helping teachers and librarians throughout his school district near Chicago. He spends his free time hanging out with his lovely wife and three adorable children.